PAPA GEE'S
HOODOO HERBAL
THE MAGIC OF HERBS, ROOTS, AND MINERALS IN HOODOO AND FOLK MAGIC

Gregory Lee White

White Willow Book

Published by
White Willow Books & aromaG's Botanica
aromaG's Botanica
Nashville, TN
www.aromagregory.com

PENDULUMS
GEM STONES
GEODES
CRYSTAL
QUARTZ
SPELLS
CANDLES
STONES
PAGAN
WITCHCRAFT
CELTIC
STATUARY
CHARMS
TAROT
LUCKY MOJO
BOOKS
GIFTS
WHITE SAGE
NAG CHAMPA
PERFUMES
ROOTS
CARDS
HYPNOSIS
ARTISAN
AMULETS
HOUSE BLESSINGS
HEALING CIRCLES
CHAKRAS
REIKI
HEALING
ROSEMARY
CARRIER OILS
SOAPS
BODY
LOTIONS
OILS
SPELLS
MAGICK
WICCA
NEW AGE
HOODOO
VOODOO
ROOTWORK
AROMATHERAPY
HERBS
LAVENDER
BATH BOMBS
TEAS
SERVING YOU SINCE 1999
aromaG's Botanica

OTHER BOOKS BY GREGORY LEE WHITE

CLUCKED – The Tale of Pickin Chicken

MAKING SOAP FROM SCRATCH: How to Make Handmade Soap – A Beginners Guide and Beyond

ESSENTIAL OILS AND AROMATHERAPY: How to Use Essential Oils for Beauty, Health, and Spirituality

LITTLE HOUSE SEARCH – A Puzzle Book and Tour of the Works of Laura Ingalls Wilder

THE USE OF MAGICAL OILS IN HOODOO, PRAYER, AND SPELLWORK

THE STRANGER IN THE CUP – How to Read Your Luck and Fate in the Tea Leaves by Gregory Lee White and Catherine Yronwode

DEDICATION

A big thank you to all of our clients and customers that have helped to make our books and products a success. We appreciate you.

AROMAG'S
BOTANICA
THE AROMAGREGORY COMPANY
EST. 1999

Largest collection in the South of artisan-made metaphysical, new age, and aromatherapy products for your spiritual practice.

Hoodoo and Witchcraft supplies, metaphysical, new age, and aromatherapy products made by artisans. **aromaG's botanica** is your source for all things herbal, aromatic, and esoteric, and a dash of occult here and there. Try our scented candles, incense, and aromatherapy oils in your own sacred space and feel the energy that awaits you.

www.aromagregory.com
www.aromagsbotanica.com

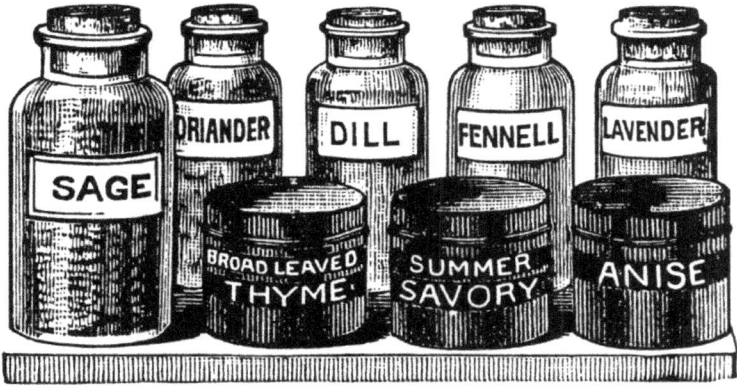

Vintage advertisement for bottles of herbs.
Peter Henderson & Co. Everything for the Garden Manual, 1898.

PREFACE

Almost all seasoned practitioners of magic will tell you that using all-natural ingredients is of utmost importance. Artificial fragrances and substances have no place in serious ritual or spiritual practice because they contain zero life-force. Herbs, roots, and real essential oils carry with them the heart of the plant they come from, its very essence.

This is the very foundation of what is known as 'sympathetic magic.' Sympathetic magic, also known as imitative magic or homeopathic magic, is magic that is based on imitation or correspondence — or both. Imitation is the idea that one thing can represent another thing and, by proxy, stand in its place. The voodoo doll, a poppet, or effigies are examples of imitation magic. For example, a lock of hair or personal item from the intended target will link them to their doll and create a magical bond. It is said that whatever happens to the doll, will also happen to that person. It is the idea that similar actions can create similar results. The rain dance is a form of imitative magic where the dancer is recreating the motions of falling rain to force the rain to fall from the sky.

Correspondence is the other aspect of sympathetic magic and is the one we turn to when using particular herbs, minerals, roots, barks, and flowers in the creation of magical oils. This concept is applied in the use of plants that are considered masculine or feminine. Some phallic- shaped roots are magically used to represent the penis while others, such as Queen Elizabeth root, resemble and are used to symbolize the vagina. The two are often brought together to bring passion back into a relationship or, more simplistically, a male root might be used to treat impotence. In the same way, a female root could be employed in fertility magic for a woman.

This philosophy carries over into the entire magical plant world. When I explain this idea to clients, I always use the rose as an example. Roses symbolize love and are given on special occasions such as Valentine's Day. It is an icon that we all recognize. But, if you were to give your sweetheart stinging nettle or a bag of clove buds, they wouldn't know what to make of it. Neither would be interpreted as an expression of love. So, sympathetically, roses carry love within them. Catnip attracts cats. Therefore, it is an herb of attraction and is used in spells to attract things to you. Ancient texts, including the Bible, described the many benefits of Hyssop. In some parts of the world, it had a religious function, and was believed to purify and "forgive sins." Christianity held hyssop in high esteem. The herb was used as a symbol of baptism and reconciliation. It is associated with purification in other religions. It is used for bruising, ear aches, tooth aches, sores, and for calming hysteria. In magical traditions, it is the number one herb used in hex removal. Just as it can holistically expel negatives and pain, it is used the same way magically — to bring the problem to the surface so that it can be expelled or banished.

When we formulate a magical oil, mojo bag, doll baby, or perform spell work, and use the proper plant ingredients for whatever condition or problem we are facing - we are putting the magic (and ourselves) in direct alignment with the wisdom and inherent knowledge of the plant kingdom. Some would say we are placing ourselves in sympathy with God (or Goddess) and everything he (or she) created.

The ingredients found in the book focus mainly on how these herbs, roots, flowers, and minerals are used in the practice of Hoodoo, Folk Magic, and Witchcraft.

G.L.W.

ADAM & EVE ROOT – Adam and Eve roots come from the roots of the Orchid plant. The 'male' roots are more elongated and are usually the older roots while the 'female' root is rounded in shape and come from younger roots. They are used in pairs for love work, specifically to make a relationship more committed and secure. For this reason, many people turn to Adam and Eve roots for strengthening a marriage.

ABRE CAMINO – Abre Camino means "road opener" or "opens roads" in Spanish. The plant, Eupatorium villosum, is found in more tropical climates such as the Caribbean, which is why it is so often used in Afro-Caribbean traditions. It is a popular herb in both Santeria and Palo, where baths are made using the fresh leaves. The dried leaves can also be used for ritual road opening baths or in sachet powders. One of the easiest ways to use Abre Camino is to simply carry it with you to remove barriers that stand in the way of your success.

AGRIMONY – Used to reverse jinxes, curses, spells, and hexes. Overcoming fear and inner blockages; dispelling negative emotions. Use as a wash or oil to increase the effectiveness of all forms of healing rituals. Used in spellwork to reveal one's true feelings.

ALFALFA – a powerful ingredient used in money drawing work. Kept in the home to ensure there is always plenty of food and money on hand. Carry alfalfa in the wallet when doing banking or meeting a loan officer.

ALKANET – The root has a history of being used as a dye. In magic, it is used for money, business matters, and gambling luck. Can also be used to counteract those people who are trying to prevent you from being successful in money matters.

ALLSPICE BERRIES – In the tradition of Hoodoo, allspice berries are carried by those who want to bring in money from gambling winnings. In witchcraft, it is used in spells of healing, determination, and energy. To protect against the evil eye.

ALTHEA – said to bring in good spirits and to increase psychic power. Also used in rituals of protection. Also known as marshmallow leaf.

ANGELICA ROOT – is widely thought to be a powerful guardian, calling upon the power of the angels. Provides strength and power to women. Used by many people for the purpose of warding off evil and used for luck in health and family. Protects children.

Angelica sylvestris

ANISE - (STAR ANISE) – is used in dream magic and can be placed under or pillow to dream of someone far away from you. When carried, it is used for psychic development and to boost powers of clairvoyance. For this reason, it is often used in psychic vision formulas. Is said to ward off the Evil Eye.

ARABIC GUM – also known as acacia gum, or simply gum arabic, it is a natural resin made of hardened sap from two species of acacia tree: Senegalia senegal and Vachellia seyal. When burned over charcoal or used as an incense ingredient, the smoke is said to repel evil and negativity from a space. Also used as offerings and summoning the dead.

BALM OF GILEAD – said to ease the pain of a broken heart and to comfort those in need. Since it is known for calming arguments it is often used in magic dealing with reconciling two people, to bring peace to a troubled marriage, and to help make a couple's home peaceful again.

BARBERRY ROOT – lay barberry across the path of an enemy to undo or lessen their effect on you. Used in protection amulets for the home and for children and is also known as Holy Thorn. Used to free yourself from the power another holds over you.

BASIL – is used in a similar way as Balm of Gilead. The two would be good mixed in a mojo bag meant for cooling the tempers of arguing lovers. It is also said to make a couple more sympathetic to the others' point of view. In Santeria, basil is used for luck and purifying baths as well as a fumigating herb, to remove spirits from a home.

BAT'S HEAD ROOT – also called Bat Nut or Devil pod, Bats head isn't actually a root but a seed pod. The reason is came to be called Bats Head 'root' is unknown. It comes from an Asian aquatic plant often called "water chestnut" or Trapa bicornis. Some say that it also resembles a horned goat or Baphomet. It is often used for protection and to ward off evil. Carry in a mojo bag for protection. Add to any spell to enhance the spell's power and carry your intentions further out into the Universe. Also used for granting wishes by burying in a pot or the ground after praying over and anointing with magical oils.

BAY LEAF – This well-known culinary herb was once used to crown Greek victors. Brings protection, success, and visions. Can magically be used as an alternative to petition paper, similar to way some write on bark. Can be used as a jinx deterrent by placing in the four corners of your property, your house, or a room.

BEARBERRY – Also known as Uva Ursi, the leaves ingested as a tea are believed to increase psychic abilities and divination in modern magic. Also used in incense and Native American spiritual smokes.

BENZOIN – known for its vanilla-like aroma, it is burned on charcoal to give one peace of mind and to bring them good luck and a sense of harmony. It is a resin from the Styrax bush, which grows in warm climates but is more abundant in Southeast Asia. Also used in cleansing and protection work, it is a good ingredient for use in a spiritual house cleansing.

BETONY, WOOD BETONY – considered an 'amulet herb' in Medieval times, betony was carried to keep away evil - both spiritually and physically. Also known as lousewort, it is used as an ingredient to reverse a witch's spell and send it back to her (or him.) Also used to bring two lovers back together who have broken up or, in other words, to reverse the problem that caused them to part in the first place. Planted in church yards to keep away evil. In Appalachian folk lore, if someone had gone almost insane for a love-spell gone wrong, the spell could be broken by taking betony and placing a leaf in each nostril, one under the tongue, in each hand, and under each foot.

BLACKBERRY LEAF – To return evil back to the one who sent it. It has properties of abundance and prosperity, so use in money spells. Sometimes is used as a protective herb. Associated with the sign of water, femininity, and linked to Brighid.

BLACK MUSTARD SEED – Used primarily to interfere with baneful magical work that others are conjuring against you. Is said to help create confusion in the mind of your enemy. Sprinkle where your enemies are sure to walk. Sometimes known as the 'seed of strife and discord.'

BLACK SNAKE ROOT – More commonly known as Black Cohosh, works as a magical barrier against all bad things from entering the home. Not only is it used to keep away negativity, jinxes, and curses, but it is also used to ward off illness and bad luck. Can be sprinkled around a house or property or steeped like a tea and used as a floor wash. Throw some black snake root into your mop water to create a solid barrier of protection on your floors then throw the mop water out the front door.

BLADDERWRACK – International travelers should carry bladderwrack with them because it is said to give protection to those at sea, or those who are flying over it. Some use it to enhance psychic powers while others use to increase business by steeping it like a tea and washing the entry way of a store. Similar to, but not the same as kelp, as many believe.

BLUE FLAG ROOT – Used in money and prosperity work, it is sometimes identified as 'snake lily.' A member of the iris family, it is used to create money drawing incense and is burned for that purpose along with other similar herbs and roots. Do not ingest.

BONESET – used to protect your health or undo curses that others have placed on you to effect your health. Wards off evil spirits when infused and sprinkled around the house like holy water.

BRIMSTONE – Brimstone, (Sulphur powder) in used in magic to prevent a hex from taking hold. Destroys an enemy's power over you. Used in hex removal and spells of banishing. An ingredient in the famed 'goofer dust.'

BUCKEYE – Carried to bring you good luck, money, and has also been used by some in divination. In the Hoodoo tradition is said to keep you in 'pocket money.' Also used as a charm for male potency. Others use in gambling and rub the Buckeye before rolling dice.

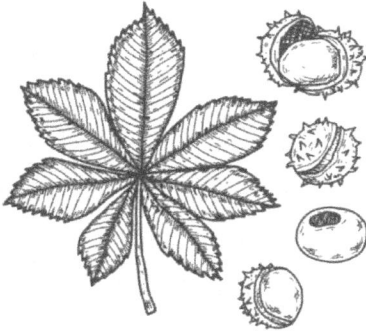

Buckeye

BURDOCK – used for protection and cleansing. String the burdock root into a necklace for protection or the larger roots can be carved into a protective amulet. Wards off negativity.

CALAMUS ROOT – In Hoodoo, calamus is used for controlling another person or a situation and is often employed in spells of domination. To bend the will of another. In the tradition of witchcraft, it is used in spells for healing and to increase the power of a spell. Do not ingest.

CALENDULA – good for dream pillows and for protection when fashioned into wreaths that are placed above doorways. Also known as 'pot marigold.' Used in home protection when blended with urine and placed at the four corners of your property. In Hoodoo, used for winning court cases.

CAMPHOR BLOCKS – many magical practitioners dissolve a block of camphor in water and place under the bed to spiritually cleanse the house. Or, for help in removing unwanted spirits. However, since it is harmful or fatal if swallowed, this isn't a good idea for those with pets or small children. Instead, crush or grate the block and use the pieces to burn on charcoal to cleanse a home - warning, very strong odor. Another alternative is to spread the crushed camphor around the property or bury (even safer for animals) at the entrance of your property.

CARDAMOM – used spells dealing with desire, lust, and all sexual matters. Some seek out recipes that include cardamom to feed someone they want to become their lover. A member of the ginger family and associated with Venus, it is no wonder that it is used for the hot, spicier side of love. For a little real-world practical magic, add a pinch of ground cardamom to red wine for its aphrodisiac effects. For spells of lust, sprinkle crushed cardamom on figural candles shaped like a penis or vagina.

CASCARA SAGRADA BARK – Used in legal matters and court case work. It is said that you should create an infusion from the bark and surround your property with it before going to court. Burning on a charcoal the day before a court date is said to increase your chances of winning.

CATNIP – used in spells for beauty and happiness, Catnip is also used to capture the heart of another and make them yours. Used for attraction spells.

CHAMOMILE – used to attract money and for gamblers to ensure winnings. Often used for sleep and meditation, but can also be sprinkled around your home and property to remove spells cast against you.

CHEWING JOHN – Also known as "Little John," it is the third in line of the 'John' roots after 'High John' and 'Low John.' Most often used in court case work and is actually chewed. The saliva that is produced is the element used in the spellwork.

CHICKWEED – for fertility, new love, or inviting a new sense of stability into an existing relationship. It was tradition in European folklore to carry a sprig of chickweed to catch a lover's eye and inspire them to remain loyal and faithful. Growing chickweed in your garden is said to bring abundance into your home.

CHICORY – used to remove all obstacles in your path that prevent you from your hopes, dreams, and aspirations. Carrying chicory on the body is said to help with gaining favors from others. Told to help with unlocking inner strength and powers. Told to make one invulnerable and bring success.

CINNAMON CHIPS – brings money to you quickly and is used in all forms of money drawing magic. When burned as an incense, it is said to raise protective vibrations. Good luck, energy, consecration, and for divination.

CLOVES – include in spells where you want another to stop gossiping about you or to keep away another's negative energy. Used to expel hostile forces, it is also used to bring in positive energy at the same time. Also used in exorcisms and to bring comfort to those grieving.

COLTSFOOT – used in spells of tranquility and peace. When burned as an incense, is thought to increase psychic visions and clear away foggy thoughts and mental issues. Use in spells that are meant to give you a fresh start.

COMFREY – often used in spells for making sure you hold onto the money you already have. Used for travel safety and is placed in suitcases to ensure your baggage is not lost. Used for car safety by creating a sachet that is hung from the rearview mirror. Wards off the evil of unknown strangers and protects from theft.

COPAL – is a resin that comes in many forms such as black, white, and golden. It is considered to be the best offering to burn for Santa Muerte and is burned on charcoal for consecration, exorcisms and banishings. Shamans would perform divination by scrying into the smoke made by burning copal, a form of ceromancy.

CORNFLOWER – also known as hurtsickle, blue bottle, blue cap, and devil's flower. It is associated with matters of sight and is said to help open up the third eye as well as bestowing the gift of seeing the Fae (witchcraft in origin.) For protection against evil spirits and to alleviate arguments between lovers.

DAMIANA – known as the 'love herb' it is especially useful in lust magic. Used to increase passion and spark an old love interest. Strong herb for use in all forms of sexuality magic.

DANDELION – for promoting psychic powers and to send messages to loved ones telepathically. Often used in dream pillows for psychic dreaming and sleep protection. Often used in divination, wishing, and calling upon spirits.

botanical graphic of
Dandelion from a 1916 medical and health book

DEVILS DUNG – Used to keep evil away from you and keep you off the radar of the law. Also used as a baneful ingredient to bring harm to your enemies or to keep them from bothering you. Has been used as an incense for protection and exorcism. Also known as asafoetida.

DEVILS SHOESTRING – In Hoodoo, it is often used for gambling and good luck. There is an old Southern belief that it should be soaked in whiskey with John the Conqueror root, then used to anoint cash before gambling. Believed to protect those who keep it near from gossip, harm, and evil.

DILL SEEDS – In Hoodoo, dill seeds are used for court case work, luck, and to keep illness away. In witchcraft, it is most often used for protection. Sew dill seeds into a sachet or bag and hang beside the front door to keep enemies away. Bathe with dill to promote lust.

DIXIE JOHN ROOT – Also known as "Low John" and "Southern John." Dixie John is used for matters that involve family life and love. Utilized to enhance your sex life and as a breakup ingredient against those who threaten your marriage. Also known as Beth root.

DOG GRASS ROOT – Can sometimes be found as 'couch grass,' which is usually used to draw in a new lover. Dog grass and dog grass root, however, is used primarily as a 'break up' ingredient. Most often used in moving candle spells for breakup work. A doll baby ingredient for controlling a lover.

DRAGON'S BLOOD – Dragon's blood is the name of the resin that comes from the plant Dracaceno draco, also known as Draconis Palm. This dark, blood-red resin is associated with the element of fire and the planet Mars. Used for protection, courage, and to gain power. Many paths believe that adding Dragons Blood to another blend you are creating or a spell you are casting will increase their potency. Can be used for cleansing a space or to banish negativity.

ECHINACEA – Also known as Purple Coneflower. A sign of strength, stamina, and prosperity, planting echinacea around the house is said to keep away financial hardships. Said to enhance and strengthen a spell.

ELDER FLOWER – protects you and your property from all intruders including robbers, the police, negative people, enemies, and evil spirits. The berries may also be used. Elder is one of the 22 trees in the Ogham, the Celtic tree alphabet. It is distinguished by five lines and is tied to the Ogham letter "R" and "Ruis." It is said that faeries live among the elder plant and help guard the door between this life and the next.

ELECAMPANE – Mixed with mistletoe and vervain, it is said to make a powerful love powder in Santeria and Hoodoo. Related to the daisy, other words for this plant are elf wort, elf dock, and Indian pipe. Said to protect against witches when mixed with mugwort and nettle.

EYEBRIGHT – for clear seeing and psychic powers. Allows one to see the truth and situations for what they really are. For help in rising above difficult situations. Sprinkle a little eyebright in your pillowcase for prophetic dreams.

FENNEL – hung in doors and windows, fennel is said to protect the home from spirits and can be carried with you for the same purpose. Used for the prevention of curses and the keep the law at bay. Also used for confidence and courage.

FENUGREEK – often used in money drawing spells and mixtures. Said to bring money into the house by dropping a few fenugreek seeds into the mop water. For prosperity, obtaining salary increases, and with help in finding money.

FEVERFEW – for safety and preventing accidents. Also for diffusing a tense or heated situation. Just as you would want to bring down a fever, use feverfew magically to reverse scenarios - from hot to cold, bad to good, indifferent to attentive. To keep others from placing binding spells on you or to remove one already in place.

FIVE FINGER GRASS – also known as cinquefoil or silverweed, it is especially for good luck in money and love. Legend says to carry a little with you if you are going to ask a favor of someone. Also used to expel evil. Ingredient in money mojo bags. Brew as a tea and wash the hands and forehead nine times to remove hexes.

FRANKINCENSE – Successful ventures, cleansing, purification. Burn for protective work, consecration, and meditation. Used as an offering at Beltane, Lammas, and Yule. Associated with self-will, self-control, or the ego.

GINGER ROOT – used in spells of success and achievement. Said to increase the power of a spell by chewing ginger root or drinking ginger tea before performing a spell or ritual. Used for money attraction, to raise the desire in a relationship, and for general protection.

GOLDENROD – Magically used for finding lost or hidden objects. Keep on the body (or in a pocket) to enhance powers of psychometry and all forms of divination. Sometimes used in money spells as a symbol of gold.

GRAINS OF PARADISE – Used for good luck, protection, making wishes and seeking gainful employment. Carry grains of paradise in your pocket during a job interview is said to bring success. Also known as Guinea Grains, many people use them exclusively for gambling.

GRAVEL ROOT – used to obtain steady work and should be carried when applying for a new job. Include as one of the main ingredients in a mojo bag in preparation for asking for a raise. Also used to remove tension from within the home.

HAWTHORNE BERRIES – primarily protective in nature, they are a good choice for creating boundaries. Use to keep a rival at bay. Drunk as a tea for those who have problems drawing a line between reality and the imaginary. For stimulating feelings of understanding and forgiveness. In England, the hawthorn is known as the mayflower tree in honor of the month during which it blooms and is said to be the first wood used for a Maypole.

HEATHER – often worn or carried as a good luck charm and is said to protect one from acts of violence or crime. Considered to be one of the best plants for summoning rain when mixed with fern. Heather has been used not only to conjure ghosts, but to open a portal to the faery realm.

HIBISCUS – used for love and marriage spells, hibiscus can also be drunk as a tea to promote sexual attraction and increase desire. Sometimes used for divination, to raise clairvoyant abilities, and to attract good spirits while keeping evil ones away.

HIGH JOHN THE CONQUEROR ROOT – Often used in mojo bags, High John is a must for African American folk magic. For mastery, power, drawing luck, masculine energy, sexuality, money, strength and is used in domination spells. Wash hands with an infusion of High John before games of chance and gambling.

HONEYSUCKLE FLOWERS – used to bind a love interest to you. When infused in oil, can be used to anoint the forehead to increase psychic vision. Placed around green candles with cinnamon and alfalfa to attract money.

HOPS – often used in dream magic to increase visions during sleep. Also to promote a more peaceful sleep while dreaming. Helps keep away nightmares.

HORSETAIL – magically used to create a barrier of protection to keep intruders off your property. Said to be useful for the summoning of snakes and snake charming. For rituals of fertility.

HYDRANGEA – often used in love magic as a replacement for Queen Elizabeth Root. Widely known as an unhexing plant that can be worn on yourself or scattered around the house. Some burn the root to rid a property of a jinx or curse.

HYSSOP – probably the number one unhexing herb, it is often used in spiritual baths to remove curses and hexes or to 'baptize' you as new when seeking a change. Purification and cleansing. Hung in the home to expel negativity and evil influences.

JASMINE FLOWERS – said to increase the power of love magic when included as one of the ingredients in your love spell. Helps to bring on new ideas and enhance prophetic dreams. Often used for attracting your soul mate in spells cast to find 'the right one.'

JEZEBEL ROOT – Jezebel Root is any of five species of Louisiana Iris, including; Iris fulva, Iris hexagona, Iris brevicaulis Iris giganticaerulea, and Iris nelsonii. Originally used by prostitutes to get paying clients, it is more modernly used to get money out of a stingy man. Many exotic dancers carry it on them to increase their tips. Another name for it is "Painted Whore".

JOB'S TEARS – used for healing, luck, and making wishes. In Hoodoo, they are gathered in groups of 7 to make your dreams come true. Can be included in mojo bags for luck and money. For protection against sorrow and emotional pain.

JUNIPER BERRY – mainly used as an herb of protection, it is also used to prevent theft. Utilized in rites of exorcism and can be used the same way to expel negative influences from your life. Also to attract a sexual partner.

LADY'S MANTLE – The patron herb of alchemy, Lady's Mantle enhances whatever magic you are performing. Used in love spells, potions, and amulets for attracting love. For connection to the Feminine or Goddess energy.

LAVENDER – a flower of friendship and harmony. While lavender is often included in love spells, it also helps to strengthen the bonds of friendship. Used to assist with sleep and rest and is also helpful in centering the mind for scrying. Worn to attract a new man or as protection from a cruel spouse. Also used in healing mixtures, to help see spirits, and is a powerful ingredient in purification baths. In aromatherapy, lavender is used for relaxation and to calm the body and mind. It is sometimes associated with the third-eye chakra, which is why it is used to center the mind for scrying and divination.

LEMON BALM – used to soothe emotional pain, especially after the end of a relationship. Also known as 'Melissa.' Helps calm the mind for those with nervous or mental disorders and can be used for clarity and focus. Soothes the mind for meditation and ritual.

LEMON PEEL – a tea made of lemon peel can be used as a wash to cleanse ritual tools and new items purchased. Also used to remove old conditions and give way for new things to appear. For purification, cleansing, and to magically cleanse the home. Evil eye protection.

LEMON VERBENA – Wear to attract the opposite sex. On the flip side, can be used to clear away old conditions and rid yourself of unwanted people. Often used in spells that help people break bad habits and addictions. Also used to cleanse a space and remove negative energy.

LEMONGRASS – is used in spiritually cleansing the home and is found in such products as Van Van oil and Chinese Wash. Said to help cleanse out jinxes and scrub away residual negative energy in a home or business. Can also be used to bathe amulets and ritual tools and is sometimes used in the development of psychic powers.

LICORICE ROOT – used in love and lust magic to ensure fidelity and to command the other person to bend to your will. For this reason, it is often used in spells that compel another to follow you or do your bidding. Used for taking control over situations and for spells of domination.

LILY OF THE VALLEY – Conscious mind, memory, mental healing, peace, tranquility, purity. Can be used in rituals/spells to stop harassment. Can be used to promote longevity in marriage. Expands feelings of peace and comfort. Memory enhancing. Do not ingest.

LINDEN – considered to be a tree of luck, healing, and rejuvenation, the branches can be hung above doorways to prevent evil-doers from entering. The flowers are used in good luck charms and mojo bags meant for strengthening love. Many of the carvings in St Paul's Cathedral and Windsor Castle are of Linden wood.

LODESTONE – has been used as a powerful amulet and Good Luck charm. It supposed to attract power, favors, love, money, and gifts. Can help to attract and brings into your life the things you want. Also known as a grounding stone.

LOVAGE ROOT – used to make one more attractive and alluring to anyone who looks upon them. To make one ache for you, mix lovage with Queen Elizabeth root and High John and bathe in for 9 days straight or take the same ingredients to make a mojo bag for love. An oil infusion of lovage is good for anointing candles of attraction. Also associated with psychic dreaming and purification.

LUCKY HAND ROOT – also called Hand of Power, it is the root of an iris plant used for money, success, prosperity, and gambling luck. Place on an altar for continuous success or use in a mojo bag along with other money luck ingredients and carry with you to bring in a continuous flow of financial luck.

MANDRAKE ROOT – Place mandrake root above the mantle in the home for protection and prosperity. Said to expel and repel demons. In Hoodoo, tie mandrake root to a doll baby and it is said to bind your love to you. Others wrap a dollar bill around Mandrake to bring in money. Also used for fertility, protection, and a gambling good luck charm.

MARJORAM – Place a bit of marjoram under your pillow to induce dreams that bring revealing information. Often used for strengthening love and protecting your relationship. Some customs include sewing a small sachet of marjoram into the wedding gown for a long-lasting and happy marriage. Associated with both Aphrodite and Isis. Use in an herbal bath for grief.

MASTER OF THE WOODS – magically about mastery and control and being in command. It is sometimes carried for protection in order to make the wearer stronger and can be used in a mojo bag for that purpose. Used when you want to be in charge of a situation.

MASTER ROOT *(Imperatoria osthruthium)* – used to gain respect and power. Carry with you to stand tall above the competition and triumphant over your enemies. Often used by athletes. For personal power. Also known as Witching roots.

MISTLETOE *(Viscum album)* – is used for protection, fertility, health, and love spells and has been used in Druidic magic for spellcasting. Kissing under the mistletoe at Christmas has ancient Roman roots where it was used in wedding celebrations during the feast of Saturnalia. Hanging it in the home is said to protect it from disease, lightening, and werewolves. *Caution: mistletoe is poisonous and should NOT be ingested, drunk as a tea, inhaled as an incense, or used on open wounds.*

MUGWORT – Burned and inhaled for psychic abilities, made into a tea to wash amulets and crystals. Place around divination and scrying tools to increase their power or near the bed to enable astral travel. Used for protection and safety when traveling.

MULLEIN – sometimes ground and used in place of graveyard dirt. Often used in dark magic spells and to raise spirits. On the flip side of the coin, mullein is hung over doorways as a powerful barrier against demons and evil spirits. Protection against nightmares. Also known as Candlewick plant, Velvet back, and Feltwort.

MYRRH – this resin is often used in rituals to heal the sick because it is said to have properties that can help people emotionally, vibrationally, and spiritually. It is one of the Biblical holy incenses and one of the three gifts presented to the baby Jesus by the Three Wise men. Burn over charcoal for strength and health. Use myrrh to help become spiritually aware.

NETTLE – powerful protector. Use nettle to break a jinx and send it back to the one who cast it. Worn as a talisman to keep negativity away. Used as an ingredient in purification baths.

NUTMEG – One of the money drawing botanicals, nutmeg is most often used in games of chance. Many use the whole nutmeg inside a money mojo bag and carry with them for gambling luck. Also used as a luck charm, they are sometimes strung with star anise and worn as a necklace.

PARSLEY – Ancient Greeks associated parsley with death, and used it in funerals and to decorate their tombs. It is said to give one safe passage to the next life or the Underworld. These origins are most likely why it is used in ritual bathing to prepare for communicating with the dead. Also used for protection.

PATCHOULI LEAF – patchouli is often associated with love and passion and relationships. In aromatherapy it is considered an aphrodisiac. But it is also strong in doing money and prosperity work - often used in money drawing oils and products or sprinkled around (or on) green candles.

PEONY ROOT – used to draw in good fortune and protect against misfortune. Worn on the body, it protects the body and soul from evil spirits and is also used to guard the home. Strung as a necklace to be worn by children for protection. Used for prosperity and success in business. Exorcism and to remove bad spirits.

PEPPERMINT – used for healing and purification, peppermint has also been used as a rub or wash on doors and furniture to expel negativity and evil. Protects the home against illness. Spread peppermint around the altar for help in performing magic.

PERIWINKLE – many spells call upon periwinkle for love, relationships, and fidelity and is sewn into the mattress to keep a married couple together. It can also be used as a binding herb to keep away those who mean you harm. For protection against witchcraft and the dark arts.

PLANTAIN – For healing, strength, and protection. Also known as Snakeweed because it is said to ward off snakes when carried in the pockets. Used in spells to ward off sickness and death.

PYRITE – often called 'Fools Gold' it is a mineral used in money magic. It guards against control and manipulation by a boss, lover, parent, or spouse. Prized by the Native Americans as a healing stone of magic. Used for good luck and much fortune.

QUEEN ELIZABETH ROOT – Also known as Orris root. Most often used to attract men and have them fall in love with the one who carries the root. Promotes popularity, success, and aids in communication.

RED CLOVER – Most often used in marriage and love spells, it also magically secures a good sex life. Used in baths for finance magic. Money, fidelity, success, luck. An infusion of red clover is said to help remove evil spirits.

RED PEPPER FLAKES – Most often used in enemy work, it is an ingredient used in 'Hot Foot' work, and some sprinkle it directly in the path of where their nemesis would walk. A traditional ingredient in souring jars as well. Magically, it is used to create an uncomfortable heat.

RED SANDALWOOD – Magical uses of red sandalwood include removing negativity, increasing opportunities and bringing success. Red sandalwood is a popular incense wood, often burned during spells for protection, healing & exorcism.

RESURRECTION PLANT – Sometimes known as Rose of Jericho. Used in magical workings to bring forth abundance and create change. When there is no water present, the plant closes into a ball and goes dormant and can remain that way for years, waiting for the presence of water, which brings it back to life and becomes green again.

ROSE PETALS – used to induce dreams of one's future love. The main ingredient used in love spells. For emotions and divinity. To build a long lasting relationship.

ROSEMARY – often used in spells of fidelity and to end jealousy. Used often for ritual cleansing by steeping rosemary in the bath water. Protection, Purification. Is also used in handfastings as a symbol of love and loyalty.

RUE – In Santeria, rue is one of the main ingredients used in purification rituals. In witchcraft and Hoodoo, it is a powerful protection herb and is often used in the crafting of talisman for that purpose. Can be sprinkled around the home or your property to protect a space.

SAGE LEAF, RUBBED – This is garden sage, not white sage. Regular garden sage is for wisdom and guidance in making decisions. White sage was not always available to all regions, so regular garden sage was burned to cleanse and purify a space. Said to help with courage and strength, as well as to weaken the ego of another.

SARSAPARILLA – used in love spells and to draw in money. Often used for health and as an ingredient for house blessings. Practiced in spells to prolong life, increase passion and sexuality, and to improve virility.

SASSAFRAS BARK – in witchcraft, it is used in love spells and romance potions. In Hoodoo, sassafras is known for increasing business and encouraging repeat customers. Also for use in money matters, especially for trying to hold onto the money you have an increase savings.

SENNA – used to draw in the love of a stranger or to intensify an existing love. Enhances the flow of love when used with other love spell ingredients.

VANDAL ROOT (VALERIAN) – use to end quarrels and create a peaceful household. Sometimes used as a replacement for graveyard dirt. Also used for darker magic to summon demons and spirits and as an ingredient in baneful spells.

VERBENA – often used for drawing in new love and breaking jinxes. Used in spells to break bad habits and addictions. Used in glamour spells and for bringing inner beauty to the surface.

VIOLET LEAF – Calms the nerves, draws prophetic dreams and visions, stimulates creativity, and promotes peace and tranquility. Violet leaf provides protection from all evil. Used for love and romance work and to heal a broken heart.

WALNUT, BLACK – used in spells of astral travel. Also for baneful work such a hexing and breakup work.

WORMWOOD – also known as Absinthe. Said to increase psychic powers, evocation, divination, scrying, and prophecy. Exorcism, binding, protection. Burned with mugwort to call upon helpful spirits. Supposed to help prevent accidents. External use only.

YARROW – used for healing, courage, self-esteem, and for overcoming fear. Taking a ritual bath with yarrow is said to increase psychic abilities. Also used to break curses.

THE MOJO BAG

Now that you know the magical meanings of the most common herbs and roots, it is time to put that knowledge into practice. While this small book was meant to be a quick guide to herbs in the tradition of Hoodoo, there was no way I could close without at least explaining how to make a mojo bag.

First, you might ask, what is a mojo bag? Basically, it is a prayer or spell in a bag. In simplistic terms, it is an amulet. In the Hoodoo tradition, we customarily use the term 'mojo bag, ' but it can be called by many other names: a mojo hand, gris-gris bag, toby, or trick bag. The word 'gris-gris' means charm or fetish. The reason behind why a mojo bag would be considered a fetish is because practitioners of hoodoo consider it to be a living thing. While a few may simply create a bag of herbal and mineral ingredients, many seasoned workers breathe life into the bag before tying it off by blowing their breath into it. So you see, these magical bags are actual charms, made so by their specific ingredients inside (and the energies of the bag's creator) that combine to form a synergistic blend of magic. Usually made of red flannel, some practitioners prefer to choose a color that relates to its use. For example, a money mojo might be green. But tradition dictates that it is almost always made of flannel. Another belief is that it is best to include an odd number of ingredients such as 3, 5, 7, 13, etc. Workers may also choose to include a certain ingredient in all of their mojo bags as a 'signature." I, myself, include lavender in all of my bags – unless a client asks me not to because of allergies. It is rather expected that the conjureman with the lavender tattoo would include this as his signature herb.

FEEDING MOJO BAGS

Creating a mojo bag is more complex than one might think. Inside there may be a variety of ingredients: herbs, minerals, bones, flowers, and sometimes personal items like a locket of hair. When made for a specific purpose or person, a mojo bag usually contains a petition (a written prayer or intention). Some people use an actual drawstring bag to create their mojo. My preferred method is what is known as a 'flaming comet' style mojo bag where a square of flannel is gathered up around the ingredients and tied off with string or twine. It should be made small enough to carry on your person. After it is created, it is fed with a liquid of some sort. While many use Florida water cologne or some other type of alcohol, I am one of those who prefers to feed the bag with condition oil — one that corresponds to the nature of the mojo bag. A love mojo, for example, should be fed with love oil. The bag is carried with you to impart its magic into your life. For the first three days, it should be kept against your skin and placed under your pillow at night. As the weeks go on and if your petition doesn't seem to be manifesting, it may be time to feed your mojo bag again. Simply rub a little oil on the bag whenever you feel it needs a magical lift.

ORIGINS, VARIATIONS, AND DETAILS

A gris-gris bag is an amulet that originated in West Africa, specifically Ghana. Like a mojo bag, it also contained a number of objects such as stones, bones, oils, and herbs that combined to provide protection against bad luck and the evil eye. When they reached America, the gris-gris changed over time. Some began to think of them as harmful tools to curse another, often being left on the tombstones of cruel slave masters or hung on buildings and homes. In Haiti, they are still considered to be positive, and bearers of good luck and have made their way into Voodoo practice. It is thought to be proper to carry a gris-gris in your left pocket. Scholars trace it to the word 'juju' the West African name for fetish or sacred object.

A nation sack is a mojo bag that is only carried by women, specifically for the purpose of controlling a man. Some debate that it is actually called a 'nature sack' and white researchers misunderstood the dialect of the black subjects they were interviewing. It appears the nation sack was not a widely known tool, with most accounts of it being made and used in the Memphis, Tennessee area. Also used to keep a lover faithful or a husband from straying, its contents are related to love, devotion, and domination. Queen Elizabeth root (orris root) is often found in a nation sack, and it is a common custom to use menstrual blood as a key element as well as the semen of the man involved.

A jackball looks similar to a mojo bag but is made and used much differently. While it also contains herbs, roots, and other components found in a mojo, those ingredients are encased in a ball of wax (or beeswax) by slowly adding wax into the ingredients and shaping into a ball. It is then wrapped in red yarn or red twine, leaving behind a long tail when complete. Jackballs are considered to be container spells, calling upon the same energy one would use to create a witch bottle. They are used as a talisman to protect against evil, to influence others, to bring mastery to the keeper of it, and can also be used for divination – the same way someone would use a pendulum. It is believed that swinging a jackball in the air charges it with power.

"When, however, one reads of a witch being ducked, of a woman possessed by devils, of a wise woman selling herbs, or even of a very remarkable man who had a mother, then I think we are on the track of a lost novelist, a suppressed poet, of some mute and inglorious Jane Austen, some Emily Bronte who dashed her brains out on the moor or mopped and mowed about the highways crazed with the torture that her gift had put her to. Indeed, I would venture to guess that Anon, who wrote so many poems without signing them, was often a woman."
— **Virginia Woolf, _A Room of One's Own_**

www.ingramcontent.com/pod-product-compliance
Lightning Source LLC
Chambersburg PA
CBHW060042050426
42448CB00012B/3104